Spotlight on

Spacecraft

Andrew Langley

Franklin Watts

London · New York · Sydney · Toronto

© 1987 Franklin Watts Ltd

Franklin Watts
12a Golden Square
London W1

Franklin Watts Australia
14 Mars Road
Lane Cove
NSW 2066

Phototypeset by Keyspools
Limited
Printed in Hong Kong

ISBN: 0 86313 630 3

Photographs:
Boeing Aerospace
European Space Age
NASA
Rockwell International
Space Frontiers Ltd

Illustrations:
Christopher Forsey
Hayward Art Group
M

Design:
David Jefferis
Janet King

Technical consultant:
Kenneth Gatland, FRAS, FBIS

Note: The majority of
illustrations in this book
originally appeared in 'First
Look' Spacecraft.

Contents

Journey into space

The first space flight was made in 1957. Since then, thousands of spacecraft have been launched. Here are some American and Russian spacecraft.

1 *Vostock*: **This carried the first person into space in 1961.**
2 *Mercury*: **The first American spacecraft to carry a person.**
3 *Gemini*: **An American spacecraft that carried two people.**
4 *Apollo Command Module*: **The American spacecraft used to land people on the Moon in 1969.**
5 *Soyuz*: **A Russian spacecraft that carried up to three people.**

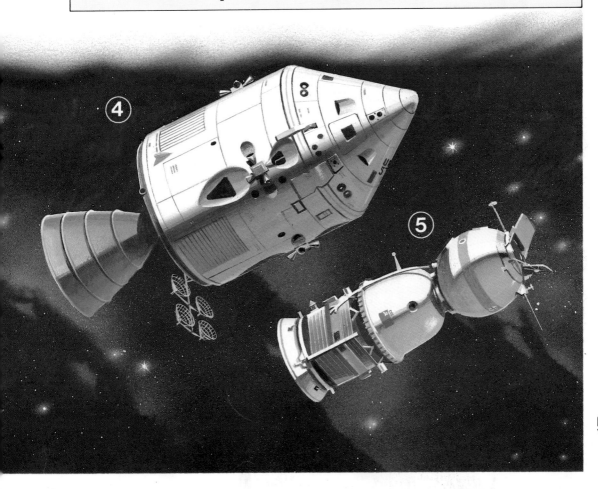

Rockets

Rockets carry spacecraft out into space. Most of them have several stages that are fired one after another. The Saturn V rocket, shown here, launched missions to the Moon.

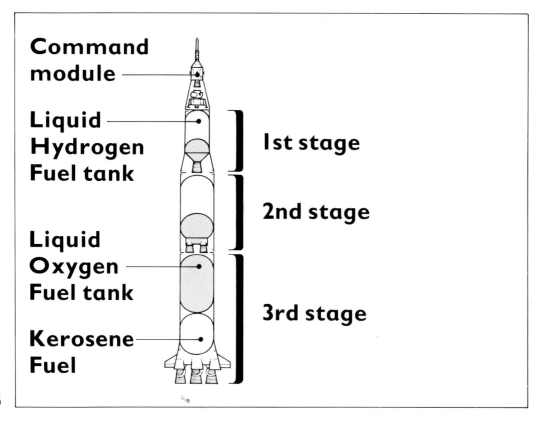

Command module

Liquid Hydrogen Fuel tank

1st stage

2nd stage

Liquid Oxygen Fuel tank

3rd stage

Kerosene Fuel

The Space Shuttle

The Space Shuttle is the first spacecraft that can be used again. Only the fuel tank is wasted. The shuttle flies back to Earth and lands on a runway.

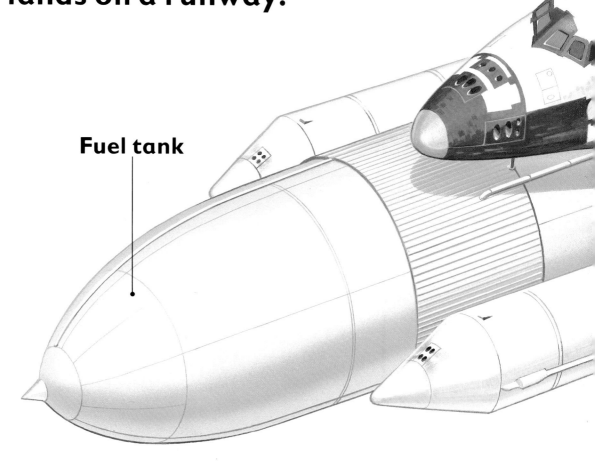

Fuel tank

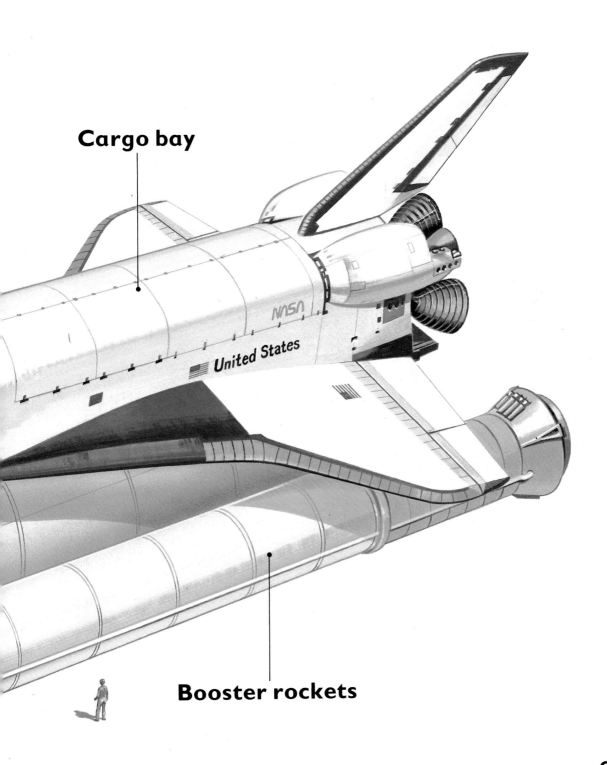

Cargo bay

NASA

United States

Booster rockets

Spacesuits

Astronauts would die in space without spacesuits. They give astronauts air to breathe. Suits also protect them from the freezing cold of space and the fierce heat of the rays of the Sun.

1. *Visor*	
2. *Backpack.* **Holds air tanks and other equipment.**	
3. *Rescue globe*	
4. *Pressurized suit*	
5. *Gloves –* **Heatproof**	

Ariane and Spacelab

Sixteen European countries have combined to build their own spacecraft. The Ariane rocket carries satellites into orbit. In 1986 it launched the Giotto space probe which flew past Halley's Comet. The European Spacelab is a flying laboratory launched by a Shuttle.

Spacelab during construction.

A satellite, in three stages, launched by Ariane.

Ariane ready for takeoff in French Guiana.

13

Satellites for many jobs

There are hundreds of satellites in orbit round the Earth. They do many vital jobs. Some relay telephone calls and **TV** programmes from country to country. Others help ships and aircraft to check their positions.

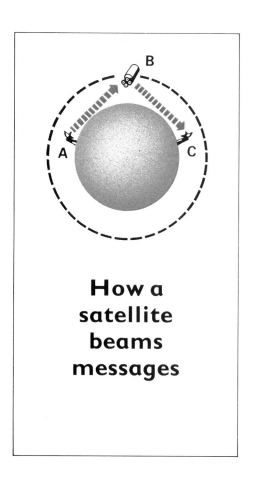

How a satellite beams messages

ATS – 6
Satellite

FLTSATCOM
Satellite

INTELSAT
Satellite

Watching the world

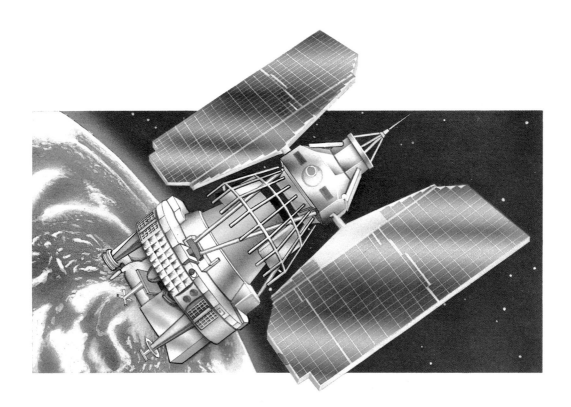

Satellites can see into every part of the world. Their "eyes" are cameras and radar scanners. The satellite shown here checks on world crops and spots sources of water under the ground.

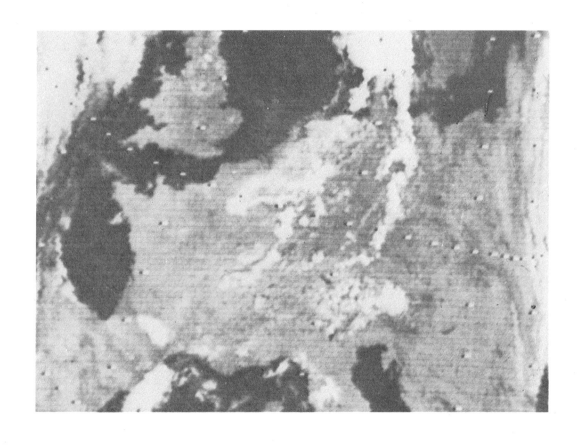

Other satellites keep watch on the Earth's weather. This picture of Europe was taken by a Nimbus satellite. The photo shows that the weather is good and that there are few clouds for most of the countries.

17

Probes to the planets

Unmanned spacecraft have visited distant planets. In 1976 an American space probe landed on Mars. It found no signs of life there.

1. *A Venera 4 Spacecraft*, which sent probes down on to Venus.

2. *A Viking Spacecraft*, which sent down an orbit on to Mars.

A Soviet spacecraft crash-landed on the planet Venus. It showed that the planet was very hot and had a poisonous atmosphere. A Mercury probe showed the planet to be very hot, with no life at all.

Into deep space

Some spacecraft have travelled to the outer edges of the Solar system. They have found strange and beautiful new worlds.

Voyager 2 passing Jupiter

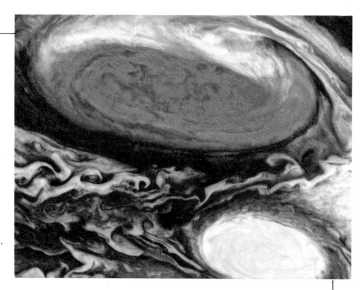

The Great Red Spot on Jupiter

Huge Jupiter was the first target.
Its most famous feature is the
Great Red Spot. Scientists think
this is a giant hurricane.
The spacecraft Voyager 2 took
pictures of Saturn in 1980. These
showed the planet's ring clearly
for the first time. Saturn was also
shown to have eight moons.
Voyager's next target is Uranus.

Space Telescope

The Space Telescope being launched from the cargo bay of a Space Shuttle.

One of the most important cargoes of the Space Shuttle will be the Space Telescope. This is due to be launched in the late 1980's as a satellite controlled from Earth. It will look at stars and galaxies that have never been seen before.

Factories in space

In the future **Space Shuttles may carry workers into space. Some will be human and some robots. Their job will be to build factories in the sky. This is what the factories may look like.**

Satellites could be joined together in clusters like this. They would replace the thousands of different satellites now in orbit. Factories and satellites should be cheap to run. They will use the free energy from the Sun.

Living in space

In the next century there may be many factories and cities in space.

There may be
scientific bases on
the Moon and
perhaps even
mining camps.
People may have
their homes
there.

Starcruiser!

The next space challenge is to travel to the stars. Some starships have already been designed. But they seem unlikely to be built. The stars are too far away. It would take many years to reach the next star.

An idea how a starship might look. Powerful radios would flash information back to the Earth, many trillion kilometres away.

**Designs
for a giant
Starship**

Spacecraft facts

The first spacecraft to go into orbit round the Earth was the Soviet Sputnik 1. It was launched in 1957.

The rocket which launched the Apollo missions to the Moon was the Saturn V. It used as much power as 50 Jumbo jets.

The first astronaut was a dog! Her name was Laika, and she was sent up in a space capsule in 1957.

Spacecraft leave a lot of litter behind. There are now about 6,000 pieces of debris in orbit round the Earth.

In 1975 two spacecraft linked in flight for the very first time. One was American, the other Soviet. Two astronauts crawled through a tunnel between them and shook hands.

The US Government is now planning to put weapons in space. These will orbit the Earth, ready to destroy any nuclear missiles launched at the USA.

The first true spaceplane is being developed in the UK. Called the Hotol, it will be able to fly from a runway into orbit and back.

Glossary

There are some technical words used in this book.
This is what they mean.

Apollo

The name given to the US space missions to the Moon. The first to land on the Moon was Apollo II.

Booster rocket

A rocket which is attached to the main spacecraft to give extra power.

Galaxy

A collection of stars, dust and gas. Our own Solar System is part of a galaxy.

Orbit

The path in which a small object travels around a larger one. The Moon orbits the Earth, and the Earth orbits the Sun.

Satellite

Any object which moves in orbit about another. The Moon is a satellite of Earth, but there are many man-made ones as well.

Solar panels

Panels which absorb the rays and heat of the Sun and turn them into energy such as electricity.

The Solar System

Our Sun and all its planets. As well as the Earth there are eight other known planets which orbit round the Sun. The System also includes satellites, comets and many other bodies.

Sputnik

The first satellite launched by the USSR. It sent out a radio bleep which was picked up around the world.

Star

A mass of gas and energy which gives out light. Millions of stars can be seen twinkling in the sky at night. The Sun is the nearest star.

Index